534
TOC

CPS – MORRILL SCHOOL

Experiments with sound.

34880030001015

534
TOC

C.l

Tocci, Salvatore.

Experiments with
sound.

$23.50   34880030001015

DATE			

CPS – MORRILL SCHOOL
CHICAGO PUBLIC SCHOOLS
6011 S ROCKWELL STREET
CHICAGO, IL 60629
02/19/2004

BAKER & TAYLOR

EXPERIMENTS WITH SOUND

A TRUE BOOK

by

Salvatore Tocci

Children's Press®
A Division of Scholastic Inc.

New York Toronto London Auckland Sydney
Mexico City New Delhi Hong Kong
Danbury, Connecticut

534
TOC
C.l
2004
23.50

The vibrations of this piano string produce sound.

Reading Consultant
Nanci Vargus
Primary Multiage Teacher
Decatur Township Schools
Indianapolis, Indiana

Science Consultants
Robert Gardner
Former Head of Science Dept.
Salisbury Schools
Salisbury, CT

Kevin Beardmore
Former State Science
Coordinator
Indiana Dept. of Education

The author and publisher are not responsible for injuries or accidents that occur during or from any experiments. Experiments should be conducted in the presence of or with the help of an adult. Any instructions of the experiments that require the use of sharp, hot, or other unsafe items should be conducted by or with the help of an adult.

Library of Congress Cataloging-in-Publication Data

Tocci, Salvatore.
    Experiments with sound / by Salvatore Tocci.
        p. cm. — (A True book)
    Includes bibliographical references and index.
    ISBN 0-516-22251-1 (lib. bdg.) 0-516-27353-1 (pbk.)
    1. Sound—Experiments—Juvenile literature. [1. Sound—Experiments.
2. Experiments.] I. Title. II. Series

QC225.5 .T63 2001
534'.078—dc21   00-052119

© 2001 by Children's Press®
A Division of Scholastic Inc.
All rights reserved. Published simultaneously in Canada.
Printed in the United States of America.
1 2 3 4 5 6 7 8 9 10 R 10 09 08 07 06 05 04 03 02 01

Contents

Cats can see very well
in the dark.

Can You Find Your Way?

Have you ever tried to find your way in the dark? Maybe you once woke up in the middle of the night, and you could not turn on any lights to see. Perhaps this happened when the electricity in your house suddenly went out because of a thunderstorm. You could not see anything, not even your hands in front of your face, because it was so dark.

None of us humans can see very well in the dark. However, there are many animals that can see well enough at night to find their way. Their eyes can let in the tiniest bit of light that is available even when it is dark.

Some animals, however, do not depend on their eyes to find their way in the dark. Bats,

Bats use sound
to move around
at night.

for example, use their large
ears to find their way during
the night. Bats listen for their
echoes. To understand what an
echo is, you can carry out experiments with something that you
make everyday—sounds.

7

What Is Sound?

You can think of a sound as waves that travel through the air. Sound waves are like the tiny waves, or ripples, that you make on water after you throw a stone into a pond. Both ripples and sound waves start in one spot and then travel out in all directions. But while you

Sound waves are similar to the ripples in a pond.

can see the ripples on a pond, you cannot see the sound waves that travel through the air. If you cannot see sound waves, how can you understand what they are like?

Making Waves

You will need:
- coiled spring toy
- measuring tape
- 12-inch ruler
- table

Ask a friend to hold one end of the coiled spring toy while you hold the other end. Stretch it across the floor about 10 to 12 feet. With your friend still holding the toy, grab a bunch of coils in your hand. Hold on to your end, but, release the rest of the coils all at once. What happens to the coiled spring toy? Did you see any waves? Sound waves travel just like the waves did along the toy.

To make the waves that traveled along the coiled spring toy, you moved your hand.

You should see the coils travel in waves along the spring toy.

Sound waves are also made when something moves.

Place the ruler on a table and slide it halfway over the edge. Press one hand firmly on the end of the ruler that is on the table. With your other hand, bend the other end of the ruler toward the floor. Then release that end quickly. Listen to the sound that the ruler makes. Experiment by placing

11

the ruler closer and farther from the edge. How does this affect the sound the ruler makes?

When you do this, you are making the ruler move quickly up and down. Each up and down movement is called a vibration. Each time the ruler vibrates, it causes the air to vibrate. Each vibration of the air makes a sound. How do vibrations produce different sounds?

12

Changing the Vibrations

You will need:
- pencil
- cork
- large stainless steel bowl or pot
- measuring cup
- water

Gently push the pencil point into the cork. With one hand, hold the bowl by the rim. With the other hand, strike the cork against the bottom of the bowl. Listen to the sound you make. Now measure 1/2 cup of water. Pour the water into the bowl. Strike the bottom of the bowl with the cork.

Listen to the sound as you strike the cork against the bottom of the bowl.

How does this sound compare with the first one? Ask someone to swish the water from side to side. While the water is swishing, strike the bottom of the bowl again. Do you hear any changes in the sound?

When you strike the empty bowl, the bowl vibrates. When the bowl vibrates, the air vibrates, which makes a sound. Also, striking the empty bowl causes the air to vibrate rapidly. These rapid vibrations make a sound with a high pitch. Musicians use the word "pitch" to describe how high or low a note sounds.

Striking the bowl with water in it produces a low pitch.

When you strike the bowl with water in it, the water slows down the vibrations. These slower vibrations make a sound with a low pitch. When you strike the bowl while the water swishes back and forth, the sound changes back and forth between a high pitch and a low pitch. Is there another way to change the pitch of a sound?

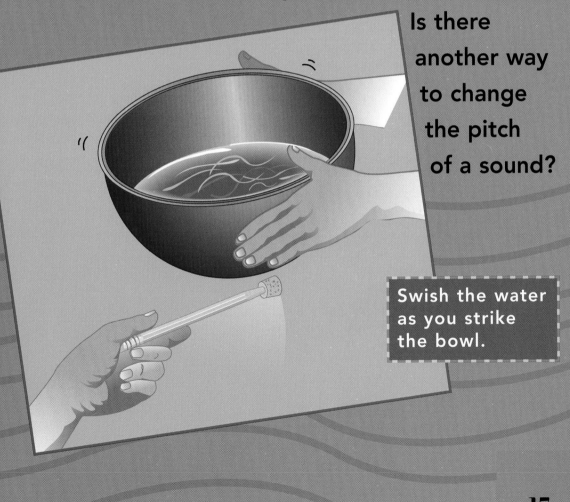

Swish the water as you strike the bowl.

Making Music

You will need:
- 5 empty glass bottles
  (24 ounce or 750 milliliter
  size is best to use)
- table
- measuring cup
- ruler
- spoon

Line up the bottles near the edge of the table. Use a measuring cup to fill one bottle with water to a level of 5 inches (12.5 centimeters) high. Pour water into the four remaining bottles.

Use the ruler to make sure that each bottle has 1 inch more water than the next bottle.

16

Each bottle should have a water level that is 1 inch (2.5 cm) different from that of the bottle next to it.

Blow across the top of each bottle, starting with the one that has the

If you use a spoon, be sure to tap the bottle at a spot above the water inside.

least water. You can also use the spoon to tap each bottle gently. Each bottle should produce a different sound. When you blow across the top of the bottle or strike it, the air inside vibrates. The bottle with the least amount of water has the most air. The more air that is present, the slower it vibrates. The slower the air vibrates, the lower the pitch. The bottle with the most water (least air) should make the highest pitch.

How Do You Make Sounds?

Playing a musical instrument is not the only way to make sounds. You can make sounds in many different ways. There is, however, one sound that you probably make the most often. This is the sound of your voice. The

You make sounds by talking!

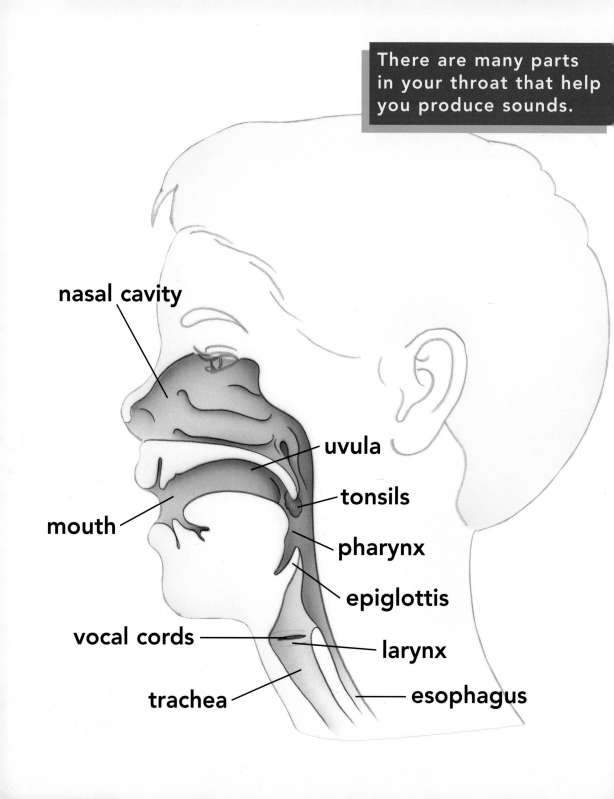

There are many parts in your throat that help you produce sounds.

nasal cavity

uvula

tonsils

mouth

pharynx

epiglottis

vocal cords

larynx

trachea

esophagus

sound of your voice is made in your throat.

Use your finger to feel the small lump in your throat. This is your larynx, or voice box. Inside your larynx are elastic bands called vocal cords.

When you talk, sing, or shout, you force air to pass across your vocal cords. This moving air causes your vocal cords to vibrate. These

Because they have a
larger larynx and
longer vocal cords,
men produce different
sounds than women do.

vibrations produce the sounds you make such as words and noises.

When a girl becomes a woman, her vocal cords stay about the same length. However, when a boy becomes a man, his vocal cords grow more than those of a girl. His larynx also gets larger. How do these differ-ences affect the voices of men and women?

Comparing Voices

You will need:
• large book
• rubber band
• two pencils

Stretch the rubber band around the book from top to bottom. Make sure that there are no twists in the rubber band. Slide the pencils under the rubber band, one at the top, one at the bottom. Gently pluck the rubber band in between the pencils with your finger. Listen to the sound. Now move the two pencils closer to each other. Notice that the length of the rubber band between the two pencils is shorter.

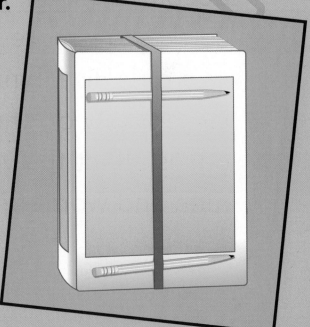

24

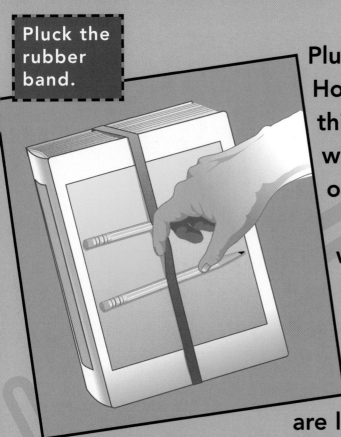

Pluck the rubber band.

Pluck the rubber band. How does the pitch of this sound compare with that of the first one?

The first sound with the longer length of rubber band had a lower pitch. Because a man's vocal cords are longer, he makes sounds with a lower pitch. The second sound with a shorter length of rubber band had a higher pitch. Because a woman's vocal cords are shorter, she makes sounds with a higher pitch.

However, all the sounds made by males and females do have something in common—they travel through the air. Can sounds travel only through the air?

Experiment 5

Traveling through Solids

You will need:
- watch or clock that ticks
- measuring tape
- wooden table
- metal tube such as one used in a vacuum cleaner

Hold the watch or clock near your ear so that you hear the ticks. Ask a friend to slowly move the watch away from your ear until you can no longer hear it. Then stop. Measure the distance between your ear and the watch.

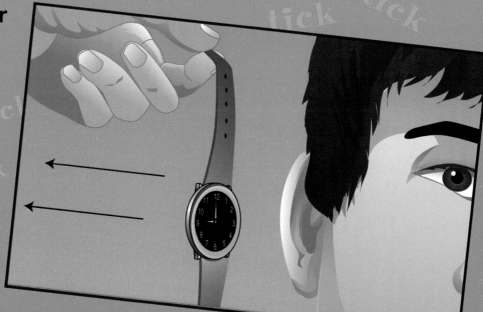

tick tick tick tick tick tick tick tick

Place your ear near the edge of a long wooden table. Have someone hold the watch near your ear so that you hear the ticks. Then ask the person to slowly move the watch away from you, along the top of the table. Stop when you can no longer hear the ticks. Measure the distance between your ear and the watch.

Place the metal tube on the table. Then place your ear against the end of the tube. Ask a friend to hold the watch on the metal tube next to your ear. Then, have the friend slowly move the watch along the tube away from you until you no longer hear the ticks. Then stop. Measure the distance between your ear and the watch.

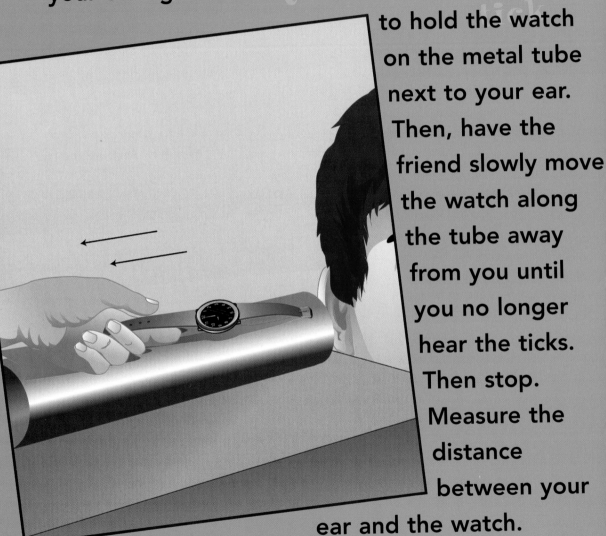

tick tick tick tick tick tick tick

You should hear the ticks farther away through the table than you do through the air. This is because sound waves travel better through solids than they do through the air. You should also hear the ticks farther away through the metal tube than you do through the table. This is because sound waves travel better through some solids than they do through other solids. Some solids can even stop sound waves from traveling. These solids are used for sound-proofing.

Some solids, like the foam used for ear plugs, can stop sound waves from traveling.

How Do You Hear Sounds?

Obviously, you hear sounds with your ears. The ear actually has three parts: the outer ear, middle ear, and inner ear. The only part that you can see is the outer ear. The outer ear traps sound waves that are traveling through the air. These

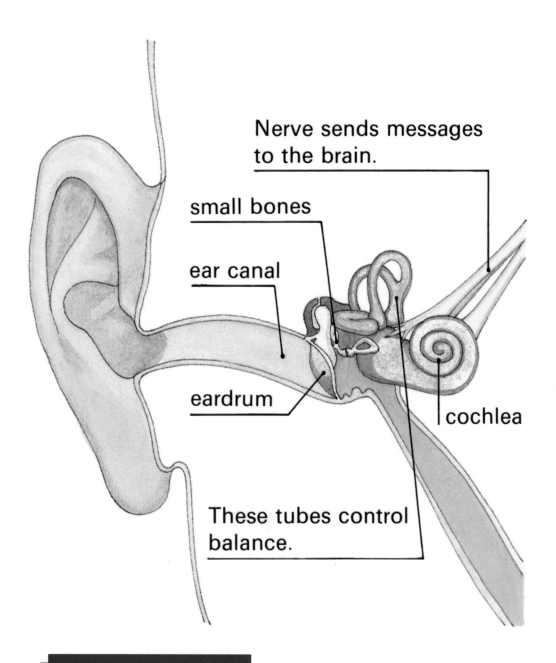

Nerve sends messages
to the brain.

small bones

ear canal

eardrum

cochlea

These tubes control
balance.

Diagram of the ear

sound waves are then sent down a canal to the eardrum. The sound waves make the eardrum vibrate.

These vibrations push against tiny bones in the middle ear. These bones make the vibrations bigger. These vibrations then make the tiny hairs in the inner ear vibrate. These vibrations of the hairs send signals to the brain. The brain finally translates these signals into sounds. Is there a way to see how the ear does its job?

Seeing the Vibrations

You will need:
- balloon
- scissors
- cardboard tube with a large opening
- rubber band
- transparent tape
- tiny mirror
- flashlight

Blow up the balloon several times to stretch it out. Let the air out and cut the balloon in half across its width. Throw away the half with the neck. Stretch the remaining piece over one end of the cardboard tube about 5 inches (12.5 centimeters) long. Use the rubber band to hold the balloon on the tube.

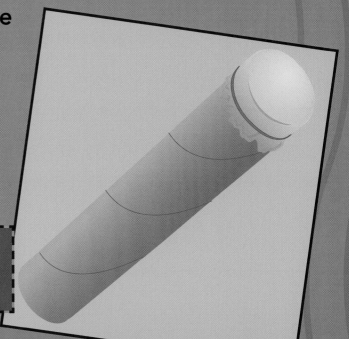

Use the rubber band to hold the piece of ballon to the tube.

Tape the tiny mirror to the balloon on a spot over the hole in the cardboard tube. Be sure not to tape the mirror to the cardboard tube.

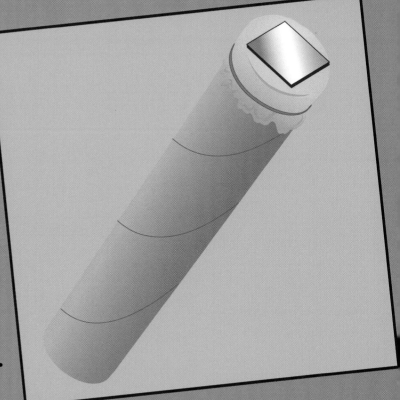

Point the cardboard tube toward a wall. Ask someone to shine the flashlight on the mirror. Darken the room. The light from the flashlight should reflect off the mirror and make a spot on the wall. While you speak softly into the open end of the tube, look at the spot.

What happens? What happens to the spot when you begin to speak louder?

Your vocal cords cause the air in the tube to vibrate. The air then makes the balloon at the end of the tube vibrate. This makes the mirror vibrate. You can see these vibrations when you look at the light spot. When you speak louder, these vibrations should get bigger.

The light from the flashlight makes a spot on the wall after it reflects off of the mirror.

Earlier, you read that bats use echoes to find their way in the dark. An echo is a sound wave that bounces off an object and returns to its original spot. The bat sends out high-pitched sounds that bounce off objects and then return to its ears. The farther away the object, the longer it takes for the echo to return. Bats use echoes to tell how far away an object is. How good are you at using echoes to tell how far away an object is?

You can hear your voice echo in a canyon as the sounds bounce off a rock wall and then return to your ears.

Listening for Echoes

You will need:
- measuring tape
- brick wall
- two pieces of wood
- blindfold

Stand 100 feet (30.5 meters) away from a brick wall. Close your eyes so that you can concentrate on listening for the echo. Clap two pieces of wood together. Listen closely for the echo. Do this again, but this time stand 500 feet (152 m) away from the wall. Do you notice that it takes a little longer for the echo to reach your ears? Practice until you can tell the difference.

To see how well you can tell the distance, put on a blindfold. Ask a friend to move you around and place you either

38

Close your eyes, clap two pieces of wood together, and listen for the echo.

100 or 500 feet away from the wall. Clap the pieces of wood together. Now guess how far away you are from the wall. If you have trouble, do not worry. It takes a lot of practice to use echoes to find your way in the dark.

Sounds travel through the air as waves. Our ears pick up these waves and send signals to the brain. The brain translates these signals into sounds. Sound waves can bounce off an object to make an echo. Bats use echoes to find their way in the dark.

Fun With Sound

Now that you have learned about sounds, here's a fun experiment for you to do. You learned that sounds can travel through solids, such as a metal tube. Another solid that sounds can travel through is a string. Find out how well sounds travel through a string.

Listening In

You will need:
- pencil
- plastic cups
- measuring tape
- string
- scissors

Use the pencil to make a tiny hole i
the bottom of each cup. Cut a piece
of string 20 feet (6 meters) long.
Thread one end of the string through
the bottom hole of one cup. Tie a knot on the
inside of the cup. Thread the other end through the
second cup and tie the string the same way.

Take everything outside.
Ask a friend to
hold a cup and wal
away from you unti
the string is tight.
While your friend is
speaking, hold the

other cup next to your ear. Can you hear your friend talking?

Thread one end of 10 feet (3 meters) of string through another cup. Tie the free end of this string around the middle of the 20-foot string. Pull the strings tight. Ask another friend to join in on your conversation. You should talk just as if the three of you were talking on the telephone. Can everyone hear what the others are saying? How many people can you include in your telephone conversation so that everyone can clearly hear the sounds?

Can you hear your friends speaking on the other end of the line?

To Find Out More

If you would like to learn more about sound, check out these additional resources.

 **Books**

Catherall, Ed. **Exploring Sound.** Steck-Vaughn, 1990.

dePinna, Simon. **Sound.** Raintree Steck-Vaughn, 1998.

Dixon, Malcolm, and Karen Smith. **Sound and Music**. Smart Apple Media, 1999.

Jackson, Dorothy, and Sally Nankivell-Aston. **Science Experiments with Sound.** Franklin Watts, 2000.

Kaner, Etta. **Sound Science.** Addison-Wesley, 1991.

Organizations and Online Sites

Science Museum of Minnesota
120 W. Kellogg Boulevard
St. Paul, MN 55102
651-221-9444
http://www.smm.org/sound/topcss.html

Check out their site where you can find activities and discussions about sound. Some of the activities you can do include making sounds with nails and studying sound waves with the help of a coiled spring toy.

Acoustical Society of America
Suite 1NO1
2 Huntington Quadrangle
Melville, NY 11747-4502
516-576-2360
http://asa.aip.org/sound.html

Log on to their site to hear a variety of interesting sounds including those made by whales.

http://members.aol.com/bats4kids/

Learn more about bats, including how they use sounds to find their food.

http://www.lucent.com/museum/timeline.html

This site allows you to explore the history of sound devices, including the telephone, microphone, and the first computers to make music.

http://www.cbc.4kids.ca/general/the-lab/do-it-yourself/9804/experiment2/default.html

Have you ever wondered why the sound of a siren changes when a fire truck passes by? This site shows you how to use an alarm clock to learn why this happens.

Important Words

eardrum part of the outer ear that vibrates when sound waves hit it

echo sound that bounces back

inner ear part of ear that sends signals to the brain

larynx voice box region of the throat

middle ear part of ear that makes vibrations bigger

outer ear part of ear that you can see

pitch how low or high a note sounds

sound wave that travels through the air

vibration back and forth movement

vocal cords elastic bands that produce sounds

Index

Meet the Author

Salvatore Tocci is a science writer who lives in East Hampton, New York, with his wife Patti. He was a high school biology and chemistry teacher for almost 30 years. As a teacher, he always encouraged his students to do experiments to learn about science. Some of the sounds he loves to hear are those made by opera singers, especially those who sing bel canto operas. He also enjoys listening to the opera sounds created by Mozart, whose *Don Giovanni* is his favorite.

Photographs ©: Elaine Mills: 31; Fundamental Photos: cover (Martin Bough), 2 (Richard Megna); Leonard Morgan: 20; Liaison Agency, Inc./Bruce Plotkin: 1; Peter Arnold Inc.: 9 (James H. Karales), 4 (Gerard Lacz); Photo Researchers, NY: 22 bottom (Carolyn A. McKeone), 7 (M.D. Tuttle/BCI); Rigoberto Quinteros: 19, 29; Visuals Unlimited: 37 (Mark E. Gibson), 22 top (Jeff Isaac Greenberg).

Illustrations by Michael DiGiorgio